LORD LONGFORD'S
BOOK OF ACCIDENTS
& MISFORTUNES
or – Hello Michael Foot!

LORD LONGFORD'S BOOK OF ACCIDENTS & MISFORTUNES

or – Hello Michael Foot!

Line drawings by Paul Watkins

SIDGWICK & JACKSON
LONDON

ISBN 0-283-98887-8

Photoset by Robcroft Ltd, London WC1
Printed in Great Britain by
A. Wheaton & Co. Ltd., Exeter
for Sidgwick & Jackson Limited
1 Tavistock Chambers, Bloomsbury Way
London WC1A 2SG

List of Contributors

The International Spinal Research Trust

No one can say how many people suffer from paralysis in the United Kingdom, but in the USA it is estimated that every forty minutes one person is paralysed through injury or illness. The frightening fact is that this could happen to anyone, and, until recently, it was believed to be incurable. Now, however, hope glimmers on the horizon: scientists specializing in paralysis resulting from spinal cord injuries believe they could be on the brink of finding new methods of preventing or minimizing the condition.

The International Spinal Research Trust works in close collaboration with other foundations throughout the world. Acting as a forum, it promotes spinal cord research with the aim of improving the functioning of the spinal cord; it explores methods of repairing or bypassing the cord by surgical or electronic means, and it investigates new drugs that could help the condition. The results of this research could revolutionize the life of those victims of spinal injury who find themselves confined to a wheel-chair. It could be a means to a new beginning – surely no cause could be more worthy?

Introduction

FRANK LONGFORD

I have been given the task of editing this anthology of mishaps and accidents as I am considered to be accident prone. In fact, I never felt this about myself until an accident overtook me. In my last year at Oxford I was invited to take part in a steeplechase known as the Bullingdon Grind, and set off on a thirty-shilling hireling with no suspicion that disaster lay ahead. My friend Aidan Crawley, an expert horseman, stationed himself at the far end of the line from me on the theory that I was bound to cause trouble.

In the event, my mount and I swerved across the field, causing one or two mishaps, though Aidan just managed to escape me. I crashed heavily enough at the first fence, causing dismay to my backers, who had made me second favourite at two to one because I had been trained by a farmer of unique standing in that part of Oxfordshire. I remounted gallantly, too excited to notice that I had lost my crash helmet – a fatal happening, as it proved. About ten fences further on I hit a telegraph pole concealed in the top of the jump by the master of the drag, who had a very slow horse but one calculated to clear telegraph poles and other obstacles.

When I came to my senses, I was standing beside my steed, and both of us were facing the jump. Naturally assuming that we had not yet surmounted it, I duly jumped it and proceeded rapidly in what proved to be the wrong direction. The ultimate winner, and I think the only finisher, Bill, later Lord Astor, was mounted on a horse called Geoffrey Austin, then priced at two thousand guineas. Fifty years later, I tremble to think of its value. Bill Astor, seeing me galloping towards him became understandably agitated. I tried to put him right: 'That's the way!', I shouted, pointing in the wrong direction. 'That's the way!', he cried, pointing in the right one. He managed to escape my clutches and cantered home an easy winner. I was led away and put to bed: I suffered from the effects of concussion for about a year afterwards.

Several distinguished contributors to this anthology have suffered mishap in the cause of sport. Tragically, Sue Masham broke her back and damaged her spinal cord irreparably upon the hunting field. She now leads the disabled lobby in the House of Lords, and it was she who suggested that all monies earned by this little book should go towards the International Spinal Research Trust. Fortunately others have been left with less permanent damage: Lucinda Prior-Palmer Green found that horse trials carry other hazards apart from the jumps; the Duke of Devonshire and Sir John Junor report ruefully upon the joys of skiing – not a sport at which the British excel – while Bob Willis, Geoffrey Boycott and Patrick Moore prove that even partaking in the game of cricket – at which the English *do* excel – can have unforeseen problems. Andrew Widdowson, one of the youngest to contribute a piece, injured his spine on the rugger field, cutting short a promising career in the game, but his delightful contribution proves that a terrible injury does not mean the loss of hope and a sense of humour.

To return to my own variegated career: 1936 saw me concussed again, this time in a fracas at a fascist meeting in the Carfax Assembly Rooms in Oxford. There are those who attribute my conversion to Socialism to my concussion in the Bullingdon incident, but it would be more plausible to link it with the fascist rally, for I joined the Labour Party soon after. I personally would prefer the idea that it was love rather than concussion and that Elizabeth – a contributor to this book – brought me into the Socialist fold. But, back to the Carfax Rooms. . . . I have never been entirely consistent in my account of my activities in the punch-up. In one version I portray myself as standing there like a persecuted saint, refusing to lift a finger in self-defence. In another, I half-killed a number of enormous fascists with the help of a steel chair wrenched from their grasp. My dear friend, Diana Mosley – who has also honoured me by contributing to this symposium – has her own version in which I don't think I figure very gloriously. I claim that I stand alone in suffering a mishap of this kind – none of my contributors has described their accidents as akin to the experiences of Paul on the road to Damascus: the politicians among them probably wouldn't let on, anyhow.

Three contributions recall war wounds: the intriguing combination of Auberon Waugh, the

10

Archbishop of Canterbury and Frank Muir. Bron, though he treats his encounter with a machine-gun lightly, was in fact very badly wounded and still suffers pain many years later. Luckily the Archbishop's war wound was less permanent in its damage, though rebukes him still with a perennially crooked toenail. Frank Muir characteristically finds hope in adversity: the tattoos bestowed upon his backside by airforce issue cutlery mark the beginning of a glorious career.

There must be people whose war record was more disappointing than mine. I have not yet encountered any. I started the war as a private in the infantry and finished as a private in the home guard. My high point, I suppose, was commanding a company in the latter in which Alan (A.J.P.) Taylor and other notables cut their military teeth. I was particularly proud of the training I supplied in musketry until one of my pupils, the Christchurch College cook, managed to fire a bullet into a school playground off the Abingdon Road in the middle of the night. It was the nearest Oxford ever came to having an air raid. The bullet ricochetted in all directions and in a moment three university dons were howling on the ground: R.G. Dundas, senior tutor at Christchurch; J.L. Austin, still credited with the most acute mind of all Oxford philosophers of the last century; and myself. I was carried away in a Black Maria to the Radcliffe Infirmary where an ultra-efficient female doctor (it could just as easily have been a man) sewed up my foot so comprehensively that bits of the sock and shoe were left embedded. Later, a line was drawn across my ankle. I was told that if the poison went any higher, the foot would be in danger.

However, the foot and I survived together.

The same part of my anatomy was in trouble again in 1947, when I was Minister for Germany. Aged forty, I prided myself rather insecurely on my fitness, though in fact with government lunches and a government car I was at least a stone too heavy. Playing squash with my private secretary, I suddenly felt an appalling impact on my right achilles tendon. It was well and truly broken, though so beautifully stitched up that I was running round Christchurch Meadows again – with more care – within three weeks. I always did my devoted secretary the injustice that it was he who had kicked me on the tendon. But quite recently I learnt that this is a permanent illusion in such cases.

As Minister for Germany I travelled to Berlin, but my arrival lacked the dignity associated with a dominant power. As the aeroplane taxied down the runway, the Germans were drawn up ready to receive me, including a band to play music of welcome. I was burning with zeal to revive the stricken country, so that when the plane came to a stop, I could not wait to get on with the job. The doors opened, but there were no stairs for me to descend. In those days the exit from a plane was nearer the ground, so it did not require an Olympic jump to make a safe landing. But as I launched myself forwards, I met the steps coming up: my glasses were knocked off, my forehead bruised and cut, the Germans were astonished, the music petered out. Somehow the Marshal of the Royal Airforce, Sir Sholtoe Douglas, later Lord Douglas of Kirtleside, was able to salute this sorry sight with impeccable gravity.

This same impeccable gravity in the face of an extraordinary mishap may be a very British trait. Some years after the Berlin incident, I occupied the honourable position of Chairman of the National Bank of Ireland, with its headquarters in Broad Street. Emerging one day on my way to lunch, I saw a bus a few yards ahead and gathering speed. Still priding myself on my fitness – a constant delusion – I raced after it, and grabbed the rail. By this time it was travelling fairly fast, too fast for me to mount it, though I hung on gamely. There came the inevitable moment when my legs were swept from under me: I was compelled to relax my grasp and lay like a stranded whale in front of the Bank of England. At that moment the Governor chose to emerge. There can be no accepted formula whereby the Governor of the Bank greets the Chairman of one of the clearing banks, lying flat on the road with the traffic passing all round him. His manner could be described as one of non-committal courtesy. Eventually I caught up with the elusive bus, by now stuck in the traffic: neither the conductor nor the passengers reacted as if anything unusual had occurred.

Humiliation is often the dominant memory which remains after an accident. Kitty Muggeridge offers a salutory tale of having her wounds tended by the very lady from whom she had stolen flowers: the reminders of her shame still clutched, drooping, in her arms. For Cyril Smith, Richard Gordon and Godfrey Smith, the humiliation is provided by the character of their mishaps: ingrowing toenails and gout are painful complaints, but like housemaid's knee and tennis elbow cause otherwise kindly onlookers to howl with mirth.

I must now push on, overlooking minor cuts, bruises and sprains. Recently, following a meeting of the council of the New Horizon Youth Centre in Soho, and still priding myself on my relative fitness, I ran down some steps in the dark, tripped over my own trousers, which had become unduly loose through careful attention to diet, and crashed into the corner of a wall. I was swept off to the Middlesex Hospital casualty ward, where I was told by the young woman doctor who stitched me up that I was the first person that evening who had not rolled off the couch through excess of indulgence of alcohol. Again, I think I can claim uniqueness with this mishap: as far as I can tell, I am the only contributor to this book who has plunged headlong down a staircase as a result of an attenuated form.

Inevitably, I suppose, a lot of the accidents related herein dwell upon broken bones and dislocations. Robert Morley, expert on stories of bricks, managed to break his ankle at the very inauguration of *Call My Bluff*; Shirley Williams found herself in a similar predicament at the inauguration of the Social Democratic Party. Cliff Richard, reveals that the Peter Pan of Pop goes in permanent fear of slipping his disc. Nigel Havers describes how, anxious to play the part of Lord Lindsay to the full in the highly successful *Chariots of Fire*, he managed to dislocate his shoulder not once, but again and again, while learning the gentle art of hurdling.

But there is another category of mishaps also related in this book, which I – very luckily – cannot claim to have experienced. Henry Kissinger, Len Murray and James Cameron all describe the frightening and painful experience of suffering a heart condition; William Davis tells of 'watching his liver' (if this had been a French symposium, such a subject would have predominated); and Clive Jenkins, with a deft side swipe at *Private Eye*, meditates on his gallstones.

And so, to the accident which led to the initiation of this book. Last winter, I had been lunching with my daughter Antonia in Campden Hill Square, and waltzed blithely down what I now realize is a very steep slope into Holland Park. It had not occurred to me that it would not only be steep but covered in ice too, and in a flash I was flat on my back. A priest and a Levite passed me by, but a young woman, possibly a nurse, helped me to my feet and escorted me back to Antonia's house. This time my destination was the casualty ward of St Thomas's, and I had broken my leg.

The following week I returned, encased in plaster and hobbling on a crutch. Two crutches were recommended, but I always found that one was less frightening. I was greeted by the huge, bearded porter with the greeting, 'Hello Michael Foot!' That famous man had recently broken his ankle and had been widely seen labouring under that affliction on television.

Hoping to claim sympathy from my colleagues at Sidgwick & Jackson, I related this experience. Sympathy notwithstanding, their thoughts flew instantly to the question as to whether there was a book in this. From the fine response to my appeal to contributors, it seems that they were, as usual, right. I have extracted some measure of revenge by persuading two of them to contribute: my editor, Margaret Willes, gives warning of enjoying

15

indulgences, while William Armstrong, Sidgwick's managing director, provides a glimpse of the violent life of the No. 19 bus.

We all hope that you enjoy this anthology, parts of which are funny, while others will provide inspiration and comfort to those who have been unlucky enough to suffer pain and illness.

THE ARCHBISHOP OF CANTERBURY

I don't usually admit to any war-wounds; but that is not strictly correct. I suppose that mine would be classed as 'self-inflicted'.

In 1942, as a young Guards officer on Salisbury Plain, I was officiously inspecting a Churchill tank and dropped a heavy engine lid on my toe. I howled with agony, but long hours of square-bashing and other well-tried forms of discipline enabled the delighted guardsmen to keep straight faces.

I was whisked off to a hospital in Shaftesbury which was full of wounded flown back from the North African theatre of operations. Amidst such battle-scarred casualties my broken toe was treated with some disdain and, though kept in for a few days, I was expected to hobble round the ward to help the overworked nursing staff – doling out knives and forks at mealtimes, and constantly being asked the embarrassing question about my wounds.

After three days I was caught by the Matron drinking whisky with the night-nurse and returned ignominiously to my unit the following morning.

The toenail never grew straight, every three years or so I have to go into the outpatients and the nail is taken off – a salutary opportunity for me to reflect on the therapeutic effects of wounded pride.

SUE MASHAM

Breaking one's back and damaging the spinal cord beyond repair means one becomes paralysed. If one always looked on the serious side of life and took all the things that only too often go wrong to heart, life would become intolerable.

Being a paraplegic I am paralysed from the chest down and do not feel or move beyond my lesion.

I have found travelling causes many unexpected incidents. While in Rome attending the Paraplegic Games, I was sitting next to a paraplegic friend in a bus. When one of our escorts came to lift us out, he picked me up. I gathered up my legs and, suspended in mid-air, found there were three legs – one belonging to that of my next door neighbour.

Because of the shortage of space, aeroplanes do not cater for people using wheel-chairs as far as the lavatory is concerned, so during long distance flights it is necessary to make arrangements to leave the aeroplane and use the airport facilities. When returning from Mauritius, we stopped at Abu-dhabi and it was arranged that I should use the lavatory. I was escorted by an Arab. I never did find out what instruction he had been given, but he never let me out of his sight. When we reached the lavatory he came inside and as I relieved myself he stood to attention. My husband, passing the door, thought he would see that all was well. He was not allowed to enter. My escort did not speak English, but I managed to buy a bracelet at the excellent airport shop, getting him to help me in my selection. My husband had by now given up making contact, as my guard performed his duties with such dedication!

CLIVE JENKINS

I sometimes look tubby in photographs: that is because I have not got a navel. It was lost rather urgently and painfully. It is always disconcerting to move off that luminous blue drug plateau, to wake up with tubes up your nose and drips irritatingly inserted in your arms.

The surgeon palmed a small jar and rattled the pigeon's egg-size stone that had been the malevolent cause of my surgery.

The gossipy press was as beastly as ever. 'Did you know he really has cancer but they are keeping it quiet?' *Private Eye* had me jumping a queue into a private room (no apology until I sued).

But one journalist benefited. Limping into the bar of Blackpool's Imperial Hotel before a Labour Party Conference, I saw a long-retired industrial correspondent then living in France.

'Dear boy, you are the reason I am here. The *Daily Telegraph* brought me back to update your obit. Don't worry, it was very kind.'

Now, there is reassurance for you. He's dead now.

Are obits the semi-colons between life and..

THE DUKE OF DEVONSHIRE

As a young man of eighteen, I went with a group of friends on a skiing holiday in Switzerland. I was never any good at skiing, partly because I am the wrong shape, but more important because I did not have the necessary skills or nerve. There is a famous ski-run called the Pas Semur, which was handy for where we were staying, so on our first day we set off. There was a ski-lift to the top of the run and my first misfortune was to fall off it. This meant I had to trudge uphill for several hundred metres through thick snow, carrying my skis. I finally got to the top and, after a rest, set off down the run, which was marked by yellow flags. To begin with all went well, but then I started going too fast for my capabilities and skied over one of these marking flags. The result was a heavy fall and a broken ankle. The folllowing day I returned to England and I have never skied again.

PRUE LEITH

Catering is a hazardous business. I once sat with two hundred other guests at dinner at a City livery hall, confidently awaiting the pheasant casserole I had cooked, I knew, to perfection. When it came it tasted of neat turpentine. We'd had the larder painted that day, and I left open pots of cooling pheasant in it all night.

Another time, dining in a City boardroom with one of our customers, I saw my host digging in the salad with a fork. He pulled out of it, first a piece of string, to which was attached a long thin metal chain, then finally out popped a rubber bath-plug. That was when I operated from a bedsitter and used to wash the lettuce in the basin.

We've served salmon mousse for pudding, think-ing it was plum fool; we've delivered cocktail bits to the wrong company, who gratefully ate them before we could get them back; we've given bacon canapés to a rabbi.

One day our delivery van door flew open in Pont Street, depositing a dinner for Beaverbrook Newspapers in the gutter.

We've dropped all the knives and forks for a party on a barge into the Thames.

I've left live lobsters destined for Princess Margaret in the tube. I've dried the icing on an almost-forgotten wedding cake with a hair dryer.

But my worst catering accident was stabbing my sous-chef. I slipped at the range, holding a sharp filleting knife. In an effort to save myself I flung my arms upwards and the next thing I knew, there he was, clutching his thigh, with blood running through his fingers. Pandemonium. The restaurant manager ordered the barman to give the poor chap a brandy. The barman (who knew his first aid better) refused to do so, so they were both off in a corner mutinying, threatening dismissal and shouting. As for me, I admit to my undying shame that I had gone into the cloakroom to be sick.

The unfortunate sous-chef was attended by the kitchen staff, all shouting and arguing, and one of them wrapped a far-from-sterile tea-towel round his leg. When I recovered my senses the poor man, pale as death, insisted on pulling up his pants because I was a woman. Arguments about tourniquets, ambulances, hospitals and tetanus injections went on, I'm sorry to say, for twenty minutes before the victim was taken off to hospital. At no time did I give a thought to our poor customers. Orders were simply forgotten. At one point a waiter mildly pointed out, 'Table Three has been waiting for half an hour', to be rebuked with,

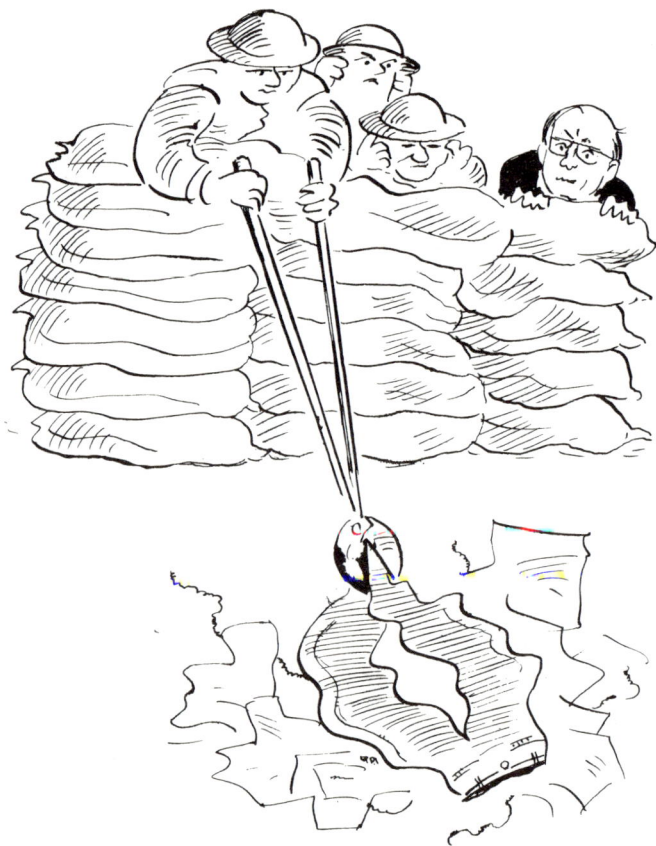

'Good God, there's a man bleeding to death here and you talk about crêpe suzettes'.

The next day I received a letter of complaint – a customer had had to wait twenty minutes for hollandaise sauce, and when it arrived it was curdled. The waiter had said, 'Well, Sir, the Chef cut his finger.' The customer was beside himself: (a) the chef had no business cutting his finger; and (b) if he had, what kind of an excuse was that? The waiter had, reasonably enough, been a little reluctant to say, 'Well, the boss has stabbed the Second Cook and the rest of them are rioting.'

GERALD KAUFMAN

The time I received a bomb in the post, I immediately telephoned the local police station. The envelope was postmarked London WC1 – the same postal district in which, a few days before, an anonymous letter had been posted telling me that I was to be murdered. It was a big envelope, the kind books are sent in. It contained something soft and thick with, in the middle of it, something hard and metallic.

A policeman came round and examined the envelope carefully. He then began in a gingerly manner to open it. I thought this most foolhardy and stood well back, though demonstrating bravery at the same time. When the envelope was open, the policeman very slowly drew out its contents. I stood even farther back. Out of the envelope came a pair of jeans: a pair of woman's jeans. The policeman stringently cross-questioned me as to

25

whether I was expecting such a piece of apparel. I assured him I was not. We both decided it was a mystery and he left, looking at me curiously.

Later, I discovered that a constituent had sent a pair of faulty jeans back to the manufacturer. She had used an envelope in which I had sent her a copy of a book I had written. The envelope in which I sent her the book was one in which another book had previously been sent to me. I had stuck a label over my address on the envelope. My constituent had stuck a label over her address. Both labels had come off, leaving the postman with only my address. That was how he came to deliver my letter bomb to me.

RICHARD GORDON

In my thirties, I used to wear flat caps and gloves with string instead of backs, driving powerful cars across the country to the alarm of the population and my passengers. A dash from Edinburgh to London ended with pain in my left foot. I sent in the car for clutch-adjustment.

It was the man, not the machine. I had gout.

Gout!

I remembered Sydney Smith – 'Oh! When I have gout I feel as if I was walking on my eyeballs.'

I remembered Thomas Hood and the naval officer –

For that old enemy the gout
Had taken him in toe!

– the menace even worse than the pun.

I remembered Gilbert and Sullivan's gondolier

with his terrible taste for tippling, which combined with gout to double him up for ever. (Gout is a very literary disease.)

Most diseases attract sympathy. Gout only derision. Everyone ascribes it to swigging port. I felt dreadfully guilty, until I remembered A.P. Herbert, writing with unflagging commonsense –

At last the happy truth is out –
Port wine is not the cause of gout;
Far more responsible for pain
Are kidneys, liver, sweetbread, brain...

I had forgotten that gout was a disorder of purine metabolism. It could occur in a teetotal, athletic monk on a diet. You took pills and forgot it.

The incident had a profound effect on my life. I never drove over thirty m.p.h. again.

MALCOLM MUGGERIDGE

Two Men in a Boat
The poet Gerard Manley Hopkins, tripping over his umbrella as he got onto a bus, is said to have muttered: 'All the universe conspires against me.' Such small catastrophes often seem more momentous than larger ones. In his novel *Resurrection* Tolstoy describes how a judge, presiding over his court, was totally preoccupied with squeezing a pimple on his face. Similarly, the Psalmist prophesies that when the Messiah comes angels will ensure that he does not hit his foot against a stone. There were to be larger hazards than this – a Crucifixion, for instance.

Looking back on some minor accidents which loomed large at the time, I came to realize that the most distracting of them all were the ones that did not happen. One such in particular has remained vividly in my memory. The time was 1925, when I was teaching at a Christian College in South India – actually, at Always in what was then Travancore and is now Kerala. The current Bishop of Colombo in Ceylon, the Rt Rev. Carpenter-Garnier, an Anglo-Catholic, was visiting the college, and I was to take him to dinner with W.E.S. Holland, a veteran CMS missionary who lived with his wife Cicely in a nearby bungalow. We could have gone by road, but I had a native canoe, rather primitive, made out of a hollowed-out tree trunk, of which I was inordinately proud. The Bishop agreed to be transported in it as Holland's bungalow, like the college, was on the bank of the Periyar River.

The Bishop turned up ready to depart in a magnificent rig – purple cassock, large shining pectoral cross, buckle shoes, biretta on his head. He was taller and more solidly built than I had realized, and, seated in the prow of my canoe, weighed it down to the point that we were almost shipping water. Seated myself at the other end of the canoe with my paddle, I by no means corrected the balance, and thought momentarily of abandoning the river and taking to the road. In the end, however, I decided to chance it, and got the canoe into mid-stream to take advantage of the current.

Every time we met a barge or one passed us, we were almost submerged by the waves it made. On the banks of the river the women at their washing, beating their saris and their husbands' shirts and dhotis against the rocks, stared at us, amazed at so august a figure as the Bishop in so paltry a craft. I kept on imagining the scene if we capsized. Surely the Bishop could swim; I saw him swimming, his beautiful cassock spread out in the water, his biretta floating away on its own, his buckle shoes sodden and heavy. One thought obsessed me – would the purple run?

In the event, we arrived at the Hollands' bungalow safe and sound, ostensibly to my great relief, but inwardly and secretly I was disappointed. Perhaps, I thought, things might take a different turn on the way back; but then the Bishop agreed all too readily to spend the night at the Hollands' bungalow, and I paddled my canoe back alone, in bright moonlight, the water luminous as I stirred it up with my paddle. It was one of those amazing Indian nights, the air miraculously still and laden with exotic fragrances, little lights from the houses flickering on either side of the river. All the way to the college I went on agonizing over whether the Bishop's purple would have run, and wonder about it still.

JIMMY SAVILE

In the world of living and working with the handicapped there are no easy-to-read rules. One learns by instinct what is needed. Here a quiet approach, there a boisterous one. A helping hand for this one is shrugged off by the next with 'I can do it, I'm not a cripple'. So eventually instinct is the answer, and then the fun can start.

Walking down the quiet corridors of Stoke

Mandeville Hospital one night, after midnight, I spy in the distance a young guy, paralysed from the waist down, making erratic progress in his wheelchair. Obviously just returned from the local pub on a late pass and much the worse, or merrier, from drink. His front wheel catches against the wall and he ever so slowly tips forward and with a

resigned sigh falls out on to the floor. He lies there laughing to himself, watching me walk towards him. We are the only two for miles around, it's so quiet. 'I've fallen out of my chair' he says. 'So it seems' says I, stepping over him and carrying on down the corridor. He rolls over in amazement and shouts 'Oi, pick me up you rotten bugger'. 'Sleep there all night you drunken sod' I reply. Having had his every need looked after for seven months he cannot believe I am now walking away from him. 'Ahhhh!' he shouts 'you dirty bastard'. 'Drunken bum' I shout back over my shoulder. All this noise has now alerted my friends, the night porters. 'What's to do?' they ask as I go into their lodge and sit down. 'A drunken para [paraplegic] has just fell out of his chair' I explain.

My pal on the floor is now stringing swear words together in amazing combination at full decibel. The porters rush off and ladle him back into his chair. They are all agreed that I am a real horse's ass.

His arrival on the sleeping ward does nothing to quieten him. 'The dirty blonde swine, I'll kill him!' and such like endearments wake everyone up. The porters tell the story and all the paras fall about in bed laughing. 'Serve you right, drunken pig' is their verdict and 'Good old Jim, he's too shrewd to have you throwing up over him'. In the excitement an illegal bottle of whisky, smuggled in earlier, is sent crashing to the floor. 'Jesus Christ!' shouts the patient 'me bleeding whisky's gone'. The ward proceeds to smell like a brewery. There is uproar and those who are not dying with laughing are starting to die for real. 'What in hell is going on here?' shouts the night sister, arriving on the scene. The porters make their escape, the joint stinks like a still, everyone is shouting impossible advice, and I am smoking a nice Havana in the quiet of the front lodge.

So, like I say, there are no real rules for living with the handicapped, but it sure do get lively at times.

HUGH CASSON

As a contributor to this anthology/symposium I am an impostor, for my life has been almost totally free from misfortune. I have never been to hospital except as a visitor, I carry no scars, and while subjected to the normal minor mishaps and humiliations of a long and busy life, misfortunes seem to have fallen more often upon my friends than upon myself, and thus are arguably – such is the guilt of the happy man – more distressful perhaps than those that occur to oneself.

Even professionally I seem to have been luckier than most. If there have been continual and common problems, delays and roof leaks and technical faults of every kind, mis-spelled foundation stone inscriptions and botched interviews, unexplained extras, there have been no collapses, no major accidents – except the destruction by an angry mob many years ago of a new office block in Cairo on its opening day. Yet, as every artist knows, every one of his works is a failure since it is not the masterpiece he hoped for, and he is doomed to live with the perpetual if challenging misfortune of creative disappointment.

Not many funny things, in fact, have happened to me on the way to the office – although once as a member (with Freddie Ayer, Rex Warner and Stanley Spencer) of a cultural mission to China we were the victims of an Intourist snarl-up in Moscow. Mistaken for a group of expert sheep-breeders, we were driven out to an experimental farm, made to don white coats and plunge our hands knowingly up to the wrist in the greasy fleeces of a new breed from the Mongolia borders. (The sheep men presumably were attending a reading of Pushkin poems.) Such is the unquestioning discipline of cultural missions that the episode, hardly to be classified as a misfortune, caused us no surprise.

As to the misfortunes of friends. . . . I knew a woman who was badly bitten in the hand by a stray two-year-old child in the transit lounge at Milan airport, and a man who in a fathers' race at his son's school sports humiliatingly broke his ankle on the starting line. There have been occasions for deprecating denials and failures of recognition. I have been mistaken in my time for Kenneth Clark, Michael Foot and Bobby Howes – misfortunes for them rather than for me – and been credited often with the design of Coventry Cathedral, the National Theatre and Knightsbridge Barracks, been asked (in 1951) to organize a display of coffin fittings and shrouds, eaten (in the belief that it was celery) the lips of a giant fish . . . all events too trivial to mention. The oddest misfortune? Well perhaps what happened to my dear friend Sir Nikolaus Pevsner, who once fell asleep – or so he told me – when *giving* a lecture.

DENIS THATCHER

In my rugby football refereeing days I refereed a game in which I apparently gave less than satisfaction to the home club.

During the following week I had a minor accident where it was reported I had been 'slightly injured'. In my mail I received the following letter:

> Dear Ref.
>
> About your accident. We were sorry to read you have been *slightly* injured.
>
> Yours truly,
>
> X Y Z

CHRISTINA FOYLE

When my father bought Beeleigh Abbey in Essex to house his ever-growing library of manuscripts, he was told that one room was haunted and that no one in living memory had slept in it.

The Abbey is a very beautiful fairytale place. The haunted room is enormous, with a great carved bed which had belonged to James I. When my father died the room was redecorated and it looked magnificent, although the slight chill and the curious sense of foreboding remained. No believer in ghosts, I decided that this was to be my room.

I shall never forget the night I spent there. At

about three in the morning I was awakened by the brilliant light of a full moon shining straight on my face through the slanting diamond window panes. Everything in the room seemed animated and the table with the water glass beside the bed was rattling. It was eerie and frightening. There certainly seemed to be a 'presence' and I had little sleep that night.

When my housekeeper brought my tea in the morning I found I had a deep bite on my neck and another on the fourth finger of my left hand, and we concluded that there must be mosquitoes in the room, so I did not sleep there again.

The following Monday when I went to Foyles my finger had turned black. We found a doctor browsing in the medical department and asked his advice. He took me straight to Hammersmith Hospital where several surgeons seemed very interested in my finger and I had a minor operation.

Apparently I had been attacked by a germ rarely seen outside Eastern Europe. My arm was in a sling for a month.

Now, whenever I see 'Count Dracula' I feel that perhaps there is more in the legends than I ever imagined.

PATRICK MOORE

During my life, I suppose I have been fairly fortunate inasmuch as I haven't been involved in many accidents. But I do remember one, which was in 1944 during my RAF career. I was flying (we won the war in spite of it!) and at one stage I managed to crack my left knee up. That meant limping around on sticks for a year or so, which didn't appeal to me in the least. I am a fanatical cricketer and my only forte is bowling. As a batsman I am a minus quantity; I have yet to reach my one hundred runs in a season (though I have got my hundred wickets many times), and at one stage in the 1950s I made eighteen consecutive ducks, all out.

Therefore, it is bowling or nothing, and I bowl my medium-paced leg-breaks off a long, leaping run with a whirlwind action which was once described in the local paper as being like a kangaroo doing the barn-dance. As a right-hander I ought to come down on my left leg, which, with a weakness there, would be difficult. But mercifully I am totally wrong-footed; all my considerable weight comes down on my *right* leg. Therefore, the fact

that it was my left knee which was knocked around proved to be unimportant.

But it was a nasty moment!

WILLIAM DAVIS

I was shattered when my doctor called after an annual check-up and solemnly warned me to 'watch my liver'. I had grown accustomed to being told that I was one hundred per cent fit. Oh, there had been a few minor mishaps now and then: I had once sprained my thumb while skiing; and my saw had slipped while I was building a fence and cut deeply into my finger, which provided a splendid excuse for giving up do-it-yourself forever. But nothing serious had happened to me since I was a child. This liver business *did* sound serious. My doctor is one of those delightful people who believe in being optimistic about everything; if *he* decides to be solemn it is advisable to sit up and take notice.

What, I demanded to know, did he mean by 'watch'? I knew nothing about the liver – though perhaps I should have done, since I have a French wife and the French hardly ever talk about anything else.

'Well', he said, 'for a start it might be a good idea to give up drinking spirits.'

Give up drinking! The man must be mad. I am a journalist, and it is a well-known fact that journalists cannot survive without a regular intake of alcohol.

'Just spirits', he said. 'You can still drink wine, though I think you should limit yourself to half a bottle a day.'

Ah, a reprieve. I was used to a bottle or two a day, but if I *had* to cut down I would give it a try. I was even prepared to give my liver a rest by sticking to Perrier for a week or so.

I started my new regime at lunchtime the following day. It wasn't easy. People are sympathetic when one is obviously sick, but seem to regard internal problems as a bit of a joke. If you hobble into the office on crutches they will express pity; if you say 'no thank you' to the proffered glass of Scotch or gin and explain that you have trouble with your liver they are liable to burst into laughter. To journalists a man who drinks nothing but Perrier water is only half a man. Your plight is seen as a challenge. 'Oh, come now', they say. 'One little drink isn't going to hurt you.' One, of course, quickly leads to two or three.

I recalled, guiltily, that I had played that little game myself when others had confessed that they had liver problems. It had seemed vastly amusing at the time; now it was infuriating. Couldn't these idiots understand that I was *ill*? Well, almost ill, anyway.

I told them, in no uncertain terms, what I thought of their callous attitude. By the following week I had found a solution which seemed a reasonable compromise: I asked for a glass of white wine and nursed it throughout lunch.

The liver is a forgiving organ – or so my doctor says – and I have gone back to drinking at least a bottle of wine a day. I still don't touch spirits: I have taught myself to despise the stuff. At the back of my mind, though, is the nagging fear that one of these days I will get another solemn call from the doctor. I cannot imagine a life without wine, but I suppose one can get used to anything if the alternative is clearly seen to be worse.

Meanwhile, I have become much more sympathetic towards people with some internal affliction. I have learned a lesson which should have been obvious a long time ago: that illness is a poor subject for humour.

ELIZABETH LONGFORD

Head-on in Ireland

It was a quiet late afternoon at Christmas-time. Dark, of course, but the road was nice and straight and not overcrowded with traffic. Thomas [Pakenham] and his family were at Tullynally for Christmas, and he had gone with me in the long yellow car, known to the children as the Yellow Submarine, to fetch his father from Mullingar Station, only twelve miles away. We were nearly back in Castlepollard, our home village, with Frank [Lord Longford] sitting at the back, Thomas driving and me beside him.

In the distance we could see the lights of an approaching car. Some way behind it was another car, also coming steadily towards us. None of us was doing more than thirty or forty m.p.h.

Suddenly the leading car began to veer towards the middle of the road. Why? There was nothing in front of it. But it still came on diagonally, now well on the crown of the road – now over the crown – now on our side of the road – now coming for us head-on.

There was absolutely nothing to be done but hit and be hit, like two bullocks in a field aimlessly butting one another. We could not pass him on his left, for the other car was coming up behind.

I knew already that one did not feel frightened before an accident, just incredibly attentive to what was going on. I had had a nasty accident about five years before and broken a bone in my back. On that occasion I had been hit behind instead of in front and had cannoned off the other car into some rubble where the road was being

40

widened. All I noticed at the time was that my Mini Traveller was being confronted by two cement posts with just space enough to get between them, and that, though totally out of control, the Traveller had travelled unerringly between Scylla and Charybdis, coming to rest in the rubble. (It was a pity that the Traveller, after its fine race, had to be put down.)

So here I was again, safe and sound, ready for my second accident.

The bang was not too bad, though Thomas's forehead was cut on his driving-mirror and my knee was bumped. Thomas sprang out with blood on his nose and indignation in his voice.

'What do you think you are doing?' he thundered. Then, pointing to the cluttered back of the other man's family jallopy, he added,

'You might have killed all those children!'

The fresh-faced young driver clambered down and said without embarrassment:

'There was a fellow behind me and I was trying to get out of his way.'

ERNIE WISE

I remember fracturing my ankle on a TV show. It was encased in plaster and so I was forced to go on to the stage with a stick. They stood me on the stage, opened the curtains and I did the act with Eric. Sort of Ern on a stick. I was like it for three weeks.

FRANK MUIR

It was January 1942, and the night, which lasted all day except for about half an hour at midday, was typically Icelandic; freezing cold and still. The road from Reykjavik to Kaldadarnes was ill-defined, as four feet of compacted snow had obliterated most of the stones and posts which marked the route, and the driver of the 15-cwt Commer truck in which we were travelling was having a nasty time.

We in the back had just completed an emotional chorus of 'You Stepped Out of a Dream' and were just beginning a cheery up-tempo version of 'The Hut-Sut Song' when the driver took the Commer into a corner a little too swiftly and we overturned.

As road accidents go it was hardly one (literally) to write home about. The Commer was a bit bent but there were no real injuries. Sergeant Braden, RSC (Musical Director of the Forces Band) sustained a fractured half-bottle of Teacher's whisky and went into a sulk, the Flag Lieutenant (compere) had torn the back of his uniform and burst into tears, but it might have been shock; Corporal Tanner, RAF (lead vocalist and womanizer of wondrous stamina) had a bang on the back of his head which for various reasons he had coming to him for a long time. I, Aircraftsman First-Class Muir, Photography Section, 931110, (self-appointed script-writer to the Icelandic Forces Broadcasting Unit) was the only one to lose blood. I had my knife, fork and spoon in my hip pocket, as was customary, and in falling back I had forked myself in the right buttock. I carried the scar – four blue dots like a tattoo – until 1958.

Cauterizing my war-wound with a dab of Sergeant Braden's whisky, I set out to seek help. Along the road I found a farmhouse and telephoned the duty officer at our base, RAF Station Kaldadarnes.

'Aircraftsman Muir reporting, Sir.' I said, 'The Commer's come to a full stop.'

He put me on a charge.

Apparently he hesitated between charging me with 'speaking facetiously to an officer whilst on duty' and 'insolence to a superior'. When I came up before the commanding officer I was disappointed to find that my crime had been whittled down to 'speaking in an un-aircraftsmanlike manner to an officer on duty'.

'Ah . . . ' said the C.O., an ex-Royal Flying Corps veteran who still wore his RFC jodphurs, 'Yes . . . explain . . . why? . . . eh?'

I explained that I was a photographer and as the squadron, though rich in Hudson aircraft, had not been issued with any cameras, I had nothing to do. So I filled in my empty days by writing pieces which were then performed over the radio, an hour of which was rented from the Icelandic Government per day so that the British occupying forces could entertain themselves.

The C.O. gaped, swallowed, and pounded on the desk with his fist for quite a while. Then: 'You mean you . . . words? Write them . . . you know, down . . . and chaps . . . on the radio, and . . . actually write them down on paper? . . . *thoughts* and whatnots?'

It dawned on me about then that the C.O., undoubted warrior though he was, or had been, was a man of few words. In fact his vocabulary seemed to consist of about a hundred and fifty words, which, when you take away everyday phrases like 'pass the marmalade' and 'does this train stop at Farnborough?', does not leave many to enrichen his conversation.

He gazed at me with awe.

'Sergeant,' he said, 'Rank . . . what he?'

The sergeant consulted his charge sheet.

'Aircraftsman First-Class, Sir', he said.

'Promote him!'

It was a warm moment.

And for me, in retrospect, it was more. It was the beginning.

KITTY MUGGERIDGE

My First Accident

The first time I recall God speaking to me in a parable, although I didn't recognize his voice at the time, was when I was about six years old. It was through an accident that the eighth commandment, Thou Shalt Not Steal, was brought vividly to my notice.

We were living at the time in a hotel in Vevey on the shores of Lake Geneva. We were the only tax exiles, the other guests were mostly political refugees of various nationalities. Among these were Prince and Princess Bariatinski and their children, whose smart sailor suits I envied. One of them, a boy of my own age, was my particular friend.

One day we were standing on the wall which surrounded the hotel grounds and overlooked the main road into the centre of the town, along which rolled a continuous stream of traffic – hay-carts, carriages and bicycles. We were discussing my smart new boots with laces, of which I was very proud, when my eye caught sight of some beautiful flowers in the garden across the road. 'Let's go and pick them', I said.

So off we dashed across the road and gathered an armful of beautiful blooms which I remember as being something like rhododendrons. Then we dashed back again. My friend got over safely, but I crashed into a cyclist, or a cyclist crashed into me, and I was knocked to the ground with blood streaming from my face. The cyclist picked me up and to my consternation bore me in his arms, still clutching the stolen blooms, into the house of the garden which we had plundered. The lady of the house kindly bathed my face. Nothing was said about the flowers. Then the cyclist carried me back, half dazed and handed me to my mother.

She was horrified and called the doctor, who patched me up. As he was leaving I heard her asking him in a distracted voice, 'Will she be disfigured for life?' . . . I'm afraid she meant physically not spiritually.

JOHN JUNOR

How I learned what life was like on crutches
It was the first week of February 1962.

There were twelve of us in the beginners' ski-class. Far below in the valley the onion-domed church, hotels and *pensions* of the Austrian village of Lech glistened like dolls-houses in the afternoon sun. Behind us lay the Kriegerhorn which we had just descended. For my part, mostly painfully on my backside.

Half a mile ahead, and just a steepish *schuss* away, awaited a welcoming mountain inn where we would have a comforting *Glühwein* before completing the descent to the village.

Nonchalantly I said to the ski-instructor, 'I'll go on ahead and order the drinks' and pushing with my sticks set off at speed. Unhappily it turned out to be uncontrollable speed.

I was going very much faster than I'd ever intended. Too fast even to sit down.

Then to my horror I discovered that my skis, instead of being together and parallel, were moving steadily and inexorably wider apart.

I realized that I, who never in my life had been able to do the splits intentionally, was about to do them unintentionally unless some miracle happened.

The next thing I knew I had gone A over T.

When they came to dig me out of the snow I discovered that in my right foot there was no feeling at all.

The aluminium sledge with handles like a wheelbarrow which they call the 'blood wagon' was summoned and a few minutes later, wrapped in a blanket and strapped in the sledge, I was being towed behind a no-nonsense peasant on skis who didn't bother making any turns on the way down. He took it straight and the only thing I could do was close my eyes and pray.

The village doctor was friendly and welcoming. No wonder. I afterwards discovered that he made enough money in a four-month session in Lech setting broken bones to keep him and his beautiful wife in comfort in the South of France for the rest of the year.

When he gently took off my ski boot I was half convinced that my foot would fall off with it.

Luckily it was a simple fibia and tibia fracture.

But it all taught me a terrible lesson. For the next ten or twelve weeks I was a prisoner in a plaster cast and on crutches.

Until that moment I had not given much thought to the plight of the disabled. It was only when I myself was disabled and forbidden to let my foot touch the ground that I realized it was impossible to board a commuter train to Waterloo on crutches. Impossible to drive a car. Almost impossible to take a bath without having someone in near attendance.

My good fortune was that my disability lasted only a few weeks. My heart goes out to all who have to suffer disabilities ten times worse and for all their lives.

JAMES CAMERON

For my first three score years I never saw the inside of a hospital. For the next few years I saw little else. To call it a crash course would be the precise truth. That was a surgeons' joke. Very humorous fellows, surgeons, when you are half-way into the anaesthetic and feel like a good laugh.

It began with an army jeep smash in Bengal. I came out of it with broken knees, ribs, and a crushed pelvis. Lucky me; the four others did not come out of it at all.

Somehow they sellotaped me together and flew me home, since Calcutta in the Bangladesh War had eight million sick and starving refugees, and was no place to write the Good Ward Guide.

Back in London they sedated me, splinted me, ECG'd me, which was where the trouble began. They found my heart was running on three cylinders, then on two, then one. It was an eerie sensation, like drowning in a dream.

From the recorded running commentary of the surgeon (emotion recalled in tranquillity?):

Now the cardiac and respiratory functions are arrest and assumed by the heart-lung machine.

That is to say, the heart and the lungs are now by-passed and taken over by the apparatus by which comparably colder blood is circulated. I remind you that a heat-exchange system is now markedly reducing the body temperature, since thereby less oxygen is required to maintain the life of a cell. And, to be sure, the life of the patient. The patient is therefore technically in suspended animation while we proceed with the mechanical surgery of the implantation. You might call this the critical part. . . .

He might call it that; I didn't call it anything. I later learned that the technical bit was the implantation of an artificial aorta called a Starr Valve, and a pacemaker to keep the apparatus ticking over. To everyone's surprise I lived, and would appear to be living still.

To my mind the resuscitation was less interesting than the by-product. When it was all over the pain was more intense and continuous than anything I had ever known before. The medics could do little about that, so I was obliged to have a go myself. It was clear I could not go on like this.

I had the idea of trying to exorcize the agony by the only sort of therapy I knew: I wrote it all down, there and then. For the first time I wrote a radio play: it was called 'The Lump'. The idea was to de-mythologize the whole mystery of cardiac surgery. 'The heart is simply a hollow muscle of extraordinary strength; it is a simple pump, pushing round two thousand gallons of blood a day . . .'. Thus I might come to terms with living for the rest of my life with a plastic valve and an electric battery, like a toy train.

Somehow the operation became a bonus. To my vast surprise the play not only took off on the BBC, it fluked the Italia Prize and had ten translations into obscure tongues, and somehow found its way on to television. I actually made a few bob out of it over the years. It was the only thing the doctors ever gave me, except, of course, my life.

That was some years ago. The intricate operation is acceptable now, if not commonplace. Fairly recently the US Secretary of State, Henry Kissinger, for instance, was suddenly found to have a defective heart, to the great surprise of many people who were unaware that he had one at all. They fixed him up and he bounced in and out of hospital in as many weeks as I had had months.

This is known as looking on the bright side, which I usually do, having once looked on the other. Every time my old thing goes Bomp-Bomb I give it a pat and say: keep it up mate, we rather need each other now.

FRANK KEATING

Injuries in Sport
The grimace is part of the drama of sport. In public there's even humour in it. It's always a giggle when the little man in the flat cap skids across the muddy field with his bucket and 'magic' sponge, sole surgical instruments to cure the felled and writhing gladiator. They get him back to the fray in seconds.

More smiles, too, as we recall such headlines as 'Mystery Rash causes Miss Barker to Scratch', or simple misprints even, like 'Stoke City Star has knee and thing injuries'. But in the locker-room, deep in the bowels of the stadium, the roar of the crowd is muffled, the greasepaint is peeled off, and the pungency now is that of a hospital corridor; it reeks of liniment and wintergreen, and the cries are a thousand variations of 'Ouch!'

The locker-room is where the ego thrashes furiously against the villain of pain, and there you will see why the pro' athlete is paid so much, why he remains special in spite of the often proper cynicism that now accompanies him in these, his salad days. The American writer, Mark Kram, made a study of locker-rooms. 'Loneliness, desperation, frustration – all ordinary emotions – are trebled in a training room', he observed. 'They cannot always be seen, sometimes only sensed – but all the time the athlete is confronting that most unordinary equation: pain and play.'

And if the injury is too great, the thoroughbred is put down in his prime. That's the fear for young men. His mind is in turmoil as his limbs thresh about down there – and he shrieks for the magic sponge. It's a short enough life as it is. The American footballer, Peter Gent, was finished by thirty-one. Announcing his retirement, he said: 'My back is ruined so I can't sit still for long. The game has given me severe arthritis in my neck for butting people with my head, and if I walk too much, my knees swell.'

Some play on for years, administering their own teeth-grinding anaesthetics by an almost heroic mind over matter. For years, the state of Denis Compton's knee riveted the British nation, just as, later, the Australians hung on to every bulletin

51

issued about Tony Roche's left elbow. You have to grin and bear it. As Merlin Olsen, the celebrated US football tackler, explained when his knee was finally laid to rest: 'Pain? It's like walking into a barnyard stinking of manure. Stand there for five minutes and you don't smell it any more. Same with my knee. It hurt. I was conscious of it. So I play at a different tempo, change my run, alter my stance, drive off a different leg.' Then, of course, the fit knee, doubly favoured, starts to creak. . . .

Willie Pep, legendary world boxing champion, summed up the neurosis of the fading athlete even more succinctly: 'As you get older, first your legs go, then your reflexes go – and, third, your friends go.' Boxing, most hateful, primitive and, I'm afraid, most irresistible of challenges, has an added sickness for the injury-prone to beware of – brain damage. Though Norman Mailer, no less, once spoke up for the noble artists: 'The popular assumption that boxers do not have brains comes from sportswriters, but then sportswriters' brains are in their turn damaged by the obligations to be clever each day. And the quantities of booze necessary to lubricate such racing of the mental gears ends up giving sportswriters the equivalent of a good many punches to the head.'

Touché. And so we're back to grinning, and bearing it: even when it's only injured pride, far away from the liniment of the locker-room. Like the resignation speech by John Ralston, coach to the Denver Broncos, 'I am quitting on account of illness and fatigue: the fans were sick and tired of me.'

Or, the very final fall of a former fighter who had once known the adulation of amphitheatres. As the *Cheltenham Echo's* headline had it the morning after the fracas: 'Ex-Boxer Battered outside Chip Shop'.

I am in this book under false pretences: I am not famous, nor have I suffered a serious accident. However, as the house editor of this book, I have heaped enough misfortune on the head of Lord Longford to justify his insistence that I should contribute.

As most of my friends would agree, my principal enjoyments in life are food, music and – I have to admit – the joys of the grape. The minor mishaps that I have encountered have featured one or more of these pleasures. Attending a ball at one of the Inns of Court, I partook of the refreshments only to lose half of one of my front teeth. I then spent the rest of the evening looking like the Witch of Endor, and was only slightly mollified by an elderly judge who, in seeking to reassure me, told me that I looked charming and put him in mind of a schoolgirl he once knew: whether this was a hark back to his dim distant youth, or a hardened case who cut a dash in the juvenile court, he did not specify.

My second accident followed hard on the heels of an excellent publishers' lunch. Overcoming my phobia about ticket offices, I had just procured a seat at the Royal Opera House to listen to a recital by the great Italian tenor, Carlo Bergonzi. In a dream, thinking of the arias to come, I didn't notice that I was wandering in the middle of the road, until I was violently nudged in the back by a car, and knocked flat. My immediate reaction, which I assume is normal for somebody who is not badly hurt, was one of intense embarrassment at my plight, spread-eagled as I was before the
54

portals of a rival publishing house. Luckily, only my amour-propre was bruised, and I was even able to endure the rigours of the amphitheatre at Covent Garden that night.

LUCINDA PRIOR-PALMER GREEN

In May 1977, riding a suitably named mare, Hysterical, I came off worse than she after we had completed a combined cartwheel over a stack of unforgiving sleepers at the Locko Park Horse Trials. I stumbled to my feet, not wholly certain of anything except that I should catch Hysterical and continue, to ensure that she had lost no confidence after our fall. I found, however, that I was surrounded by uniformed ambulance men and women.

Firmly they steered my totter to the ambulance and, 'No', I was not allowed to continue riding. As I climbed into the white van, I heard and felt a well remembered click around the collar bone area. The tightness of my right arm made it clear what had happened.

A few bumpy minutes later the ambulance pulled up outside the first aid tent. Eventually the door was opened and I wandered out of the back. Several unattended somewhat groggy steps later I tripped over the corner guy rope of the tent. The attendants looked round to find me sprawling, injured shoulder first, towards the, by then, familiar Derbyshire turf.

Thereafter the remaining six yards of my journey inside the tent to a chair, were carefully monitored.

I never knew what happened after that because

much to my amazement and certain disgust, I remember being unable to fight off a descending curtain of blackness as I quietly slid into a faint, probably back onto the same poor shoulder.

MELFORD STEVENSON

Many years ago, when my old friend Gilbert Beyfus was gravely ill, the case in which I was appearing 'went short' and I arrived back home in the early afternoon, thinking to enjoy a short siesta. However my dear wife, who has never much held with time mis-spent, said: 'You're always saying you want to go to see Gilbert – why not now?' So I put on my bowler hat again, got the car out, and set off for the wilds of Surrey. Having lost myself down a number of winding lanes I finally arrived via several muddy and gated fields at the Beyfus home where I was warmly welcomed by Gilbert's devoted wife. However, when glowing with virtue, I was ushered into the invalid's room I was deflated to be greeted with the words 'As if a death bed wasn't bad enough without seeing you, Melford'.

It is fair to say that we then had a happy – to me anyway – hour or so reminiscing about ourselves and our cases over some generous refreshment. It was the last time I saw him and I took away the memory of a very brave man as well as a formidable advocate.

DENIS NORDEN

All my own minor accidents have been of too distressing a nature to be treated lightheartedly, ranging as they do from spinning myself clean off a swivel chair, to spilling hot coffee on my lap at a nudist picnic. However, I do have a friend who was once run over by a mobile library van – and he swears that, as he lay in the roadway groaning, a lady leaned out of the driver's window and said 'Sh!'.

ROBERT MORLEY

As one of the team captains of the inaugural programme of the long-running BBC game, *Call My Bluff*, I waited in the foyer of Television House for my lot to arrive, and ran forward in a totally unnecessary gesture to assist the late Dame Sybil Thorndike out of her cab. I tripped over the kerb and landed flat on my back with my foot sticking out at a curiously disturbing angle.

'It's a Potts fracture,' announced Jonathan Miller. 'Don't move.'

'Good of you, Jonathan,' I murmured, 'but I wonder if you would be so kind as to send for a Doctor?'

'I am a Doctor,' he replied, 'and I've sent for an ambulance.'

'I think it better,' I told him, 'to move the relatives away while I am being put on the stretcher. Brave as I am, I may not be able to resist a low moan when the time comes.'

'It won't hurt,' he assured me and in point of fact it didn't.

The ambulance proceeded at a snail's pace.

'Ring the bells,' I admonished, 'let's get a move on.'

'It's just round the corner,' they told me, 'We need to get our breath back.'

HENRY KISSINGER

For about a year and a half, I had constant pain in my right shoulder and neck from two separate injuries. At one point I went to a doctor about the shoulder and he wanted to operate, thinking it was an orthopaedic problem. I was working on my book, so I didn't want to face surgery. Then, last fall, an acute pain developed right next to it, down my shoulder blade and across my right collar bone. I made an appointment at Massachusetts General Hospital. They found there was something amiss

orthopaedically, but not enough to explain the severity of the pain. The doctor suggested I return for a stress test to see if the heart might be involved.

A week or two later there was a blizzard in New York. I had to abandon my car at the UN and walk about six blocks to my apartment. On the way the pain became excruciating. Also, for the first time, I noticed a shortness of breath. Nancy called Dr W. Gerald Austen, an old friend and one of the country's noted heart specialists. He arranged for me to return to Mass General for two days.

They did two things: a bone scan to check the orthopaedic part and a stress test to determine the condition of my heart. I passed the bone scan and flunked the stress test appallingly. I mean, really dangerously. They then took an angiogram and found that one artery was one hundred per cent blocked. So I had only two functioning, and one was sixty per cent blocked. They felt I'd better get a heart operation as quickly as possible.

My first reaction was incredulity. I've never been sick – except for 'flu or a cold – a day in my life. I'd never stayed in a hospital except for an appendix operation thirty years ago. Now I had an unbelievable schedule ahead of me, and I began bargaining with poor Austen to see whether he could operate on 15 July, then I remembered I had something on 20 July – well, maybe 1 August, I thought. Then I remembered I wanted to go to Africa in September . . . and to China in October. I was trying to treat surgery like an event that had to be put on my schedule. This was, of course, nuts, because the penalty of delay is a heart attack.

They acted wisely. The doctors didn't argue

with me until they had all the facts and the angiograms showed the blockages. Then they said there was no way I could last until 15 July without risking a major heart attack. They said that this operation doesn't really change your life, but a major heart attack changes everything. There was no further controversy. I said, 'Let's do it as quickly as possible.'

I have no way of knowing what caused my heart problem. I've never smoked, I almost never drink. I always had the idea that I had enormous endurance. When more work needed to be done, I just added three or four hours to the day or worked through the night. Four or five hours' sleep was average. I certainly hadn't been taking care of myself, and didn't watch my food intake. I didn't spend enough time on exercise. The best I ever managed was an occasional swim or walk. I suppose all these factors contributed, but I don't know.

The night before surgery I was working on some fifteen thousand words of copy for *Time* while the nurses were prepping me, shaving my chest and putting this yellowish antiseptic solution on my body. One of my surgeons came in, and I said 'I'd like to talk to you, but I've got to get this material to *Time* tonight.' I was antagonizing the guy who had my life in his hands! Still, I talked to the *Time* editor for an hour and a half. What else could I do? The alternative was to lie around contemplating the operation.

All the doctors said that I was going to have a hellish two days after the surgery, but that I'd never remember a minute afterwards. It's true I had a bad two days, but I remember it all. You come out of that operation with some twelve lines and drainage tubes connecting you to such things as IVs, the electrocardiographic and blood pressure monitors. Because of the respirator, you have a gag down your throat and cannot make a sound. That's not pleasant.

It was a new experience for me to be absolutely dependent on people. I couldn't even turn over without nurses helping me because the pain would have been too great. I had to be turned regularly, and my vital signs had to be taken every half hour. So I would just doze off, and then somebody would wake me up, give me a pill or take my pulse. All I wanted was to be left alone. They asked Nancy what music I hated most. She said rock 'n roll, so they put on some rock 'n roll music just to get the juices flowing again. Then they put a movie on television. I was still so doped I couldn't fully understand it. But they kept me alert through that first night.

One of the least pleasant aspects of recuperating is that they make you cough after they've broken your breast bone in order to get at your heart. They make you cough seven or eight times a day to prevent pneumonia. One person wrote to me that you think the terrible time is when you cough: in fact, it's that first sneeze. My first sneeze was no joke, but luckily it came three weeks after surgery.

I owe a lot to Nancy for getting me through the first days of my recovery. She stayed with me the whole time, when things were the most painful. I don't really know why I've healed so well. I credit some outstanding doctors, a basically strong constitution, and my refusal to be an invalid. I received calls from Secretary of State Haig and from four American presidents – Reagan, Ford, Nixon and

Carter. Considering what I said about Carter in the last elections, his was an act of great human generosity! Three days after the operation I was having visitors and trying to stay as close to my normal concerns as I could.

I weighed more than two hundred pounds at the time of the operation but have lost nineteen since and have another fifteen weeks to go. All the things I like are bad for me. I like sausages. I like whipped cream. I like lots of eggs. Lately I have been eating a lot of salads – not my favourite – and chicken. Still, I can't do better than lose three or four pounds a week. But I have to keep it off, I don't want to go through this again.

There is no question that when you learn that you have physical limits, that is something important in your life to think about. But although surgery was a painful experience, there is not going to be a traumatic change in my life. The day before I returned to hospital for my check-up, I took all the doctors in my case and their wives, seventeen people, to dinner, and broke their hearts by breaking my training in the most egregious fashion.

(Interview with Gail Jennes from *People* magazine, 5 April 1982. Reprinted by kind permission.)

CYRIL SMITH

The only really serious injury that I have suffered (thank God) was as a child when I was tripped in the school yard. I cut my knee, a piece of tarmac

63

entered the bloodstream, poisoned my kidneys, and I was in bed for months. Much of me (though I confess not all) that you see today, is due to that incident. Later I became Chairman of the Rochdale Education Committee, and I always then *insisted* that school playing areas must either be grass or properly covered!

I can tell you, however, that some three or four years ago I suffered from an ingrowing toenail. The doctor examined it, and decided that I must go to hospital to have part of the nail removed. Now I just cannot stand people playing with my feet – I once fainted at the chiropodists!

'Doctor', says I, 'you'll have to give me a general anaesthetic.' 'What, for a toenail?' says he, 'A local will do.' 'No', says I, 'I could not stand to watch you playing with my toe.'

'Cyril', replied the doctor, 'if you are laid on a

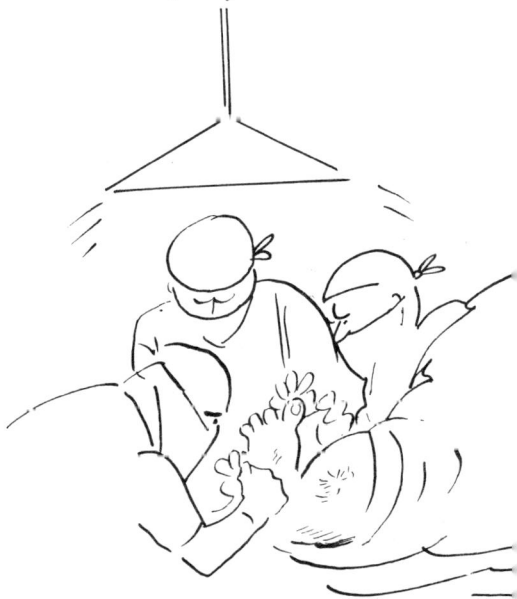

stretcher, there is no way that you would see what I was doing to your toe.'

I leave it there, and hope there will never be an occasion, about which I could write further!

AUBERON WAUGH

All my life I have been accident prone. My father used to attribute this to a desire to draw attention to myself. The first occasion on which I drew attention to myself in this way was simply by running into a gatepost at the age of five – I was carried, unconscious, three miles home and bear the scar to this day. Next, I shot myself six times with a machine-gun while I was in the army in Cyprus. I had misunderstood the mechanism and

was trying to correct what I thought was a reluctance on its part to point where I wanted it. Most recently, I fell off a camel in the middle of the Western Desert on a visit to a monastery outside Aswan. I attributed this last misfortune to the curse of Tutankhamen, whose mortal remains I had just visited for the first time, and who was reputed to have cursed my family ever since my great-uncle, the fifth Earl of Carnarvon, dug him up in 1923.

But I suspect that the real reason for all these accidents was indeed the desire to draw attention to myself. Even nowadays, I am approached by kind people offering me the chance of telling the story of my accidents for publication in little books, which certainly would not happen if I had avoided the gatepost, stood clear of the machine-gun, or stayed put on the camel.

BOB WILLIS

Injuries and me
Considering I have all the gaucheness of a camel, I often blush inwardly when I am described as an athlete or an international sportsman. I may have been lucky in terms of possessing a will-to-win or sheer determination, but when the gods were handing out the portions of grace and fluid movement, they did not linger very long at my door. When I watch fast bowlers like Michael Holding or Dennis Lillee, or see Bob Taylor perform a stumping with sumptuous ease, I can appreciate how aesthetically pleasing the game of cricket can be.

Unfortunately I have done little to enhance its beauty – my long, pounding run-up, my flailing windmill action are the hallmarks of an 'effort' bowler: I am the cart-horse to the Gold Cup winner that is Holding or Lillee. Yet I am proud that I made up for my technical and visual defects by sheer hard work and the realization that every season is a bonus to me.

Despite media generalizations, I have been relatively lucky during a career of bowling fast throughout more than a decade for England. I have been written off more times than I care to remember, but there is a grim satisfaction in proving the sceptics wrong. Only twice have I had to return early from England tours abroad – although I admit that each time I was worried about my future in the game and, indeed, whether I would again be able to walk properly.

In 1975, I had major surgery on both knees after returning home from Australia. Without being too dramatic, I might have died: I developed a pulmonary embolism – in effect a blood clot – and although I knew little about the events, I came through because of superb surgical skills. Looking back on it, perhaps all that gin in my bloodstream was also a contributory factor!

When your life as well as your career has been in jeopardy, you subsequently have a couple of behavioural choices: you can either vow never again to take things seriously; or you can try to make things happen in your favour. I chose the latter – I embarked on a reorganization of my training schedule. I knew that my time in the top flight would be limited because of the strains of my unorthodox bowling action on an unimpressive, angular physique. With the help of the England physiotherapist, Bernard Thomas, I developed a new attitude to the pain barrier; I dragged myself out of bed on dank, drizzly mornings to run five miles while the bulk of Birmingham folk were still yawning and scratching themselves. It worked, both on a physical and a mental level: no longer was I worried about answering the captain's call at the end of a long day in the field. I could keep going and I experienced a mixture of professional pride, pleasure, gratitude and profound relief.

The same emotions crowded through my brain on a sunny spring morning in 1981. I had been told that I could, after all, continue to play top-class cricket, that the injury to my left knee was not as serious as many believed. I had come home a fortnight earlier from the West Indies, in pain after slipping on greasy turf. I had to start thinking about other ways of earning a living if the surgeon's opinion went against me – what could a fast bowler on the scrapheap do with himself for the rest of his life? Luckily such considerations were shelved as I received the all-clear. Between the operation and the start of the 1981 season – a matter of a month – I trained furiously hard. I was goaded by the press headlines ('One Tour Too Many For Big Bob') that had ushered me home early from the Caribbean. The incentive to prove the media wrong lurks in the breast of most top-class sportsmen and I am no exception. I was lucky – the soft grounds of May allowed me to ease the knee through the crucial early weeks, and the plethora of limited overs matches meant I did not have to bowl too many long stints until my confidence was high enough. By the time we came up against the Aussies I felt fine and never bowled better for so consistent a period than in that 1981 series.

A year later, I have never felt fitter; my running programme is smooth and I have no qualms about my knees. I cannot crouch down in the slips or spring sharply but that stems from the wear and tear of being a fast bowler rather than chronic knee trouble. I can compromise on things like that as long as the chance of playing for England is still there.

To the injured and the disabled, my advice is simple – do not give up, make your luck change by effort and mental strength. I was lucky to have friends on hand to galvanize me in my dark times, but ultimately I realized the responsibility for recovery rested on my shoulders. Heaven knows what my physique will be like in years to come – I am sure I shall pay the piper for all the contortions and effort involved in bowling fast. Yet it has been worth the pain. I have made it on effort – and at any level such a quality compensates for so much else.

REGINALD BOSANQUET

Carrying on with Mr Stone

Some three years ago, I was visiting a friend, Bernard Stone, in hospital. He was suffering from trouble with his jaw and was imprisoned in a wire device which made him look exactly like a television set, or rather an ITV aerial. It was New Year's Eve and had been raining without cease all day. At last it stopped and I set out (I had no raincoat). As I was waiting for a taxi, a vast German container-wagon came past and, running through a large puddle, sent up a wall of water which quite literally soaked me from the waist down. There was nothing to do but carry on: I was not near my home.

When I arrived at the hospital I found Bernard ('Where's the man who looks like a television set?') and to my delight he had been given a cubicle at the end of the ward, owing to his assistance with its duties.

'Bernard', I said, 'Have you got a radiator?'

'Of course. Why?'

'Because I have been flooded by a lorry while

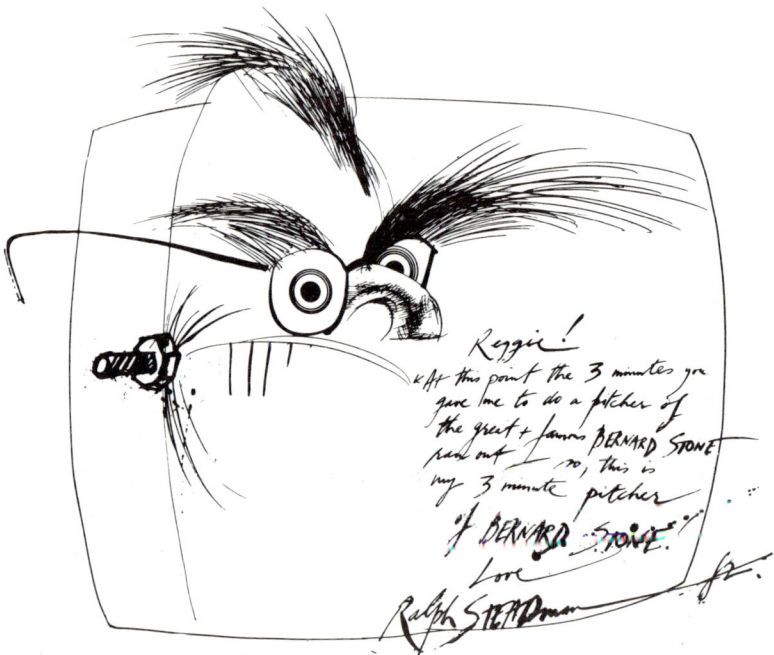

Reggie!
«At this point the 3 minutes you gave me to do a pitcher of the great & famous BERNARD STONE ran out — no, this is my 3 minute pitcher "of BERNARD STONE"
Love
Ralph STEADMAN

waiting for a taxi and my trousers are literally soaking wet.'

'Take them off, Reginald, and we'll dry them.'

I hurriedly did so and handed them to him.

At that moment, the Matron came in. She looked at us.

'Matron,' I said, 'You must believe that I'm an orphan of the storm' and explained what had happened.

'Oh, dear,' she said. 'I'll put them in the hot-cupboard for you. You just carry on with Mr Stone.'

SHIRLEY WILLIAMS

Breaking a leg was not the unmitigated disaster I would have expected it to be. There have been some improbable benefits.

First of all, it was good to be reminded of the friendliness and professionalism of the doctors and nurses in the hospital where I spent ten days. Second, my immobility gave me time at least to talk at length to my friends, a pleasure I have enjoyed too little in the last few years. Third, I have learned a bit about patience: that healing takes time and cannot be forced, that everything takes longer to do, and that taking things slowly has its compensation. I also understand better what it is to be disabled: that negotiating a kerb can be as difficult as climbing a mountain; and finding yourself without food, when the nearest shop is an impossible hundred yards away, can mean a day of hunger.

It was worth it on reflection, but once is enough.

BASIL BLACKWELL

My Dear Frank,

Your very kind letter and note have given me much pleasure. I am grateful but perplexed, for I do not know how to respond to your suggestion that I should write a few lines about my 'mishap', for I haven't had one except to be born ninety-three years ago. On that account I am beginning to join the company of the three-legged as a precaution lest I should tumble in the street.

Last year I spent a week in the Acland Nursing Home under the suspicion of incipient pneumonia; they soon put that to rights. It was a comfortable experience – just precautionary I believe – and the Acland has about the best cuisine in Oxford now. I did fall down and bruise my hip-bone but the bruise worked its way out in four or five weeks without treatment. So I am bound to disappoint you. If I get a chance to do better I will let you know!

Yours most kindly,

Basil

DIANA MOSLEY

I know that slipping on a banana skin is an old and favourite joke. It has never happened to me, but if or when it does it will give pleasure to many. My mother used to say how much people enjoy telling about disasters, and that if she got an incurable cancer, she would be comforted (up to a point) to know that each person who heard the news would have a happy time passing it on, with a virtuous expression of sorrow on her face. I have put *her* face because men are less apt to feel that particular courage in another's troubles. It is unfashionable to notice, let alone comment upon, any differences whatever between the sexes, but this is something I have observed during my long life.

To be asked to write about one's accidents, 'humorously if possible' is the limit; of course the accident may amuse others, but it is hardly ever amusing to oneself. Never mind, here goes. The only real accident I ever had was on a lovely warm July evening. I was dining out, and had made a plan to go with my future husband, Oswald Mosley, to a house he had near London for the weekend. We were to have started at midnight. While I was dressing for dinner he telephoned and said he couldn't make it until next morning, so I asked him to have a door left unlocked at his country house and said I would drive myself down and sleep in the cooler air. At dinner my neighbour was Lord Beaverbrook, a stimulating companion at all times, full of political gossip and amusing spite of all descriptions. It was great fun and I stayed fairly late, then went home and changed, got my spaniel and drove away.

I had not gone far when disaster struck. At a rather dangerous corner near the circular block of flats in Lowndes Street an enormous Rolls Royce bore down upon me and hit me amidships. The next thing I knew was that I was being dragged out of the car, and then I was lying on the pavement with my head in a policeman's lap. 'Where is my dog?' I asked. 'Oh, he's all right', said the policeman.

Consciousness came and went. I heard a woman's voice; she was saying to her companion, 'Don't look, it's too horrible.' It took several seconds for it to sink into my fuddled brain that what was horrible was me. I was wearing white clothes and they were soaked in blood.

I was lifted into an ambulance. 'Please take me home' I said. 'I live nearby, 2 Eaton Square; please bring my dog.' 'Yes, yes,' they said. They didn't want me to be agitated and I believed they had taken my spaniel home, whereas in fact he was at the police station all night, suffering from shock and wondering where I was, and he was nervous for the rest of his life.

They carried me up the steps into St George's Hospital, and I was laid on a table. A young doctor lifted my swollen eyelids and shone a torch into my eyes. They sewed up the cuts on my face with what felt like tarred rope. 'Sorry about this,' said the young doctor, 'they've locked up the thin thread.' The pain woke me. 'May I telephone?' and he said, 'Certainly not.' Then I said, 'If I promise not to scream at each stitch will you let me telephone?' He replied, 'There isn't a telephone, at least there is but it's on the wall and you can't stand'. 'Carry me then,' I said, and they did and I rang up Mosley, who answered in a very sleepy voice. It was 2 a.m. I was just about done for but I managed to say: 'I'm quite all right.' I was terrified lest he should see in the morning papers that I'd had a crash. In fact it missed the morning editions, and appeared in the evening papers next day.

I was put in a ward with women who were recovering from operations. Lying awake amid their grunts and snores, my face hurt. My brother

74

Tom was allowed to take me home, as no bones were broken. The women were quite sorry to see me go; they said they loved accidents, they were bored with each other and it made a nice change. 'Dana, your face!' said Tom when he saw the bandages. Poor Mosley, waiting for me; I can never forget his dear, anxious expression. I felt strangely confident that all would be well, and somebody, I think it was Lord Moyne, my former father-in-law, sent for Sir Harold Gillies who removed the tarred rope and operated on my broken nose and jaw when the swelling had gone down.

According to Mosley, the police report said I had been driving with my dog on my lap, and gazing at the stars. Probably my dog had crept onto my lap when we were hit, and was found there by the police. The stars, needless to say, were Mosley's invention when he wished to embroider and tease. This accident happened in 1935. I was very lucky to have Sir Harold Gillies, and not to go through life looking like a prizefighter.

JEREMY THORPE

During the 1970 General Election I flew into Birmingham by helicopter at 9·15 in the morning and landed on a football field. Although the rotor blades were still whirring, a crowd of about fifteen hundred surged towards the helicopter. My first wife Caroline screamed and pointed to a tuft of human hair blowing across the field. Having scalped a member of my audience, there was no doubt that

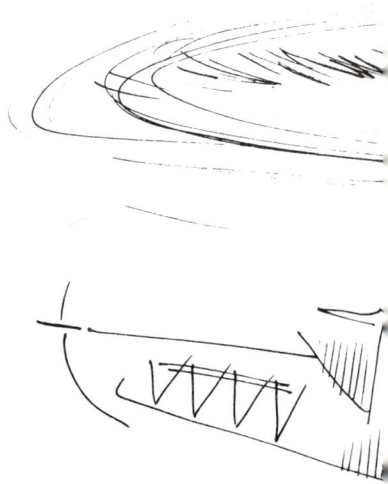

he or she would be dead. My reactions were painful and detailed. Should I call off campaigning for the day as a sign of respect and mortification – or even for two days? Should I visit the next of kin? Could the inquest be put off until after polling day? Presumably the press would do nothing else but make constant repetitious references to the accident. Likewise, I supposed that I should have to shoulder all the blame and would be told that in the first place I should never have travelled by helicopter during an election.

We both emerged rather green to look for the corpse. This time the Fates were kind, and we were to discover that a young lady had been wearing a wig which got caught in the upstream of wind. She survived; the wig was trampled underfoot.

ANDREW WIDDOWSON

After sustaining a serious spinal injury whilst playing rugby for my college, St Catherine's, at Oxford, I was able to continue my studies for a post-graduate certificate of education, recommencing in October 1981. Teaching practice started in January 1982 and for me this took place at a school in Abingdon. While doing teaching practice, I was continually amazed at the pupils' seemingly total acceptance of my teaching them from a wheel-chair. They were never afraid to ask questions about me and always appeared to accept the answers as quite logical. There was a lull in one of the mathematics lessons (there were many, actually!), and one of the members of the class came up with a question.

'Did you break your back, Sir?'

I replied in a way so as not to make it sound too dramatic, 'No, actually I broke my neck.'

Back came the questioner with, 'Does that mean that everything below the break is affected?'

This was, in fact, a fair representation, and I replied accordingly. The lull in the maths lesson continued for a few moments, when back came another question, 'Did it affect your brain, Sir?'

I explained that it had not, adding that my brain was above my neck, anyway. I thought that this was a fairly logical answer, and found that it had been received as such when back came, 'Golly Sir, it's just as well you didn't break the top of your head!'

RICHARD BAKER

It is tempting Providence, but nonetheless true, to say that so far I have suffered no sudden or serious injury. However, when I was in my first year as an undergraduate at Cambridge in 1943, I did suddenly fall victim to acute appendicitis. The manner in which I was treated caused deep shock in my parents, though as far as I was concerned it was pleasant enough.

Confronted with the need to make an immediate decision, the authorities at my college, Peterhouse, lost no time in sending me to the best available nursing-home and booking the best (and most expensive) surgeon. Only when the operation was already in progress were they able to make contact with my parents, and my mother came post haste to inspect the casualty.

She was greatly relieved to find that the operation had been a success, but since we were a family with little or no cash to spare, and what little there was had already been committed to the business of keeping me at Cambridge, my mother's relief was tempered with horror at the luxurious surroundings in which she found me. Her financial alarm in no way decreased when she learned that, although I was in no danger, there were complications which would necessitate my staying in the nursing-home for perhaps three or four weeks.

As things turned out she need not have worried. The college, full marks to them, accepted total responsibility for their decision, and, when they realized our situation, paid all the bills. But I shall never forget that look on my mother's face, torn between happiness that all was well and her obvious conviction that the same result could have been produced on the National Health.

WILLIAM ARMSTRONG

A Chinese Coat

My very minor misfortune occurred during the cold spell shortly before Christmas 1981. I had been effectively insulated from the cold by a most magnificent quilted blue coat, which I had bought in Peking the previous month for about £6.

One evening, on my way back from work, I was standing on the ground floor of a No. 19 bus, when I heard a voice upraised in obscenity. Such occurrences are not unfamiliar on a No. 19 bus as it proceeds through north London, and I did not take too much notice. It seemed that an uncouth, swarthy and thick-set man was berating a black woman for jostling him and for being black.

The bus stopped, the obscene berator got off. My impression was that the black woman moved to a seat in the front of the bus. A few seconds later the bus stopped at a set of traffic lights. The man had obviously been brooding on his grievances, and as a consequence had pursued the bus, leapt aboard and rushed up the stairs saying: 'I'm going to get that black —.'

I had hoped that when he had drawn a blank on the top of the bus, he would give up his quest for vengeance, as I realized that I was the only line of defence between him and his intended victim. Unfortunately, when the demented sub-human returned to the ground, he spied his quarry at the other end of the bus. As he rushed up the bus his way was blocked by me. I attempted to restrain him in a calm and reasonable manner, pointing out that as he wasn't going to be allowed to go any further, he might as well get off the bus now, etc. He tried ineffectively to strangle me, and I was relieved to find he was no stronger than I was. He then attempted a few left and right hooks, but these were easily parried. He removed his coat and attacked again. We wrestled up and down the bus, and during this bout my beautiful warm, satisfying coat was ripped.

After this passage of arms, we stood eyeing each other, panting, when it occurred to me that it was time Authority intervened. I saw the bus conductor looking nervous and neutral at the end of the bus. I shouted: 'Stop the bus and get the police'. My fellow-travellers on the ground floor, who had also shown no inclination to intervene, repeated these words in chorus. Whether this demonstrated that I had won the hearts and minds of the bus people, or the word 'police' had unpleasant connotations, my assailant decided to give up. He shouted a few more insults, mainly accusing me of sexual perversions, and then dismounted in the area of Sadler's Wells, going muttering off into the night.

In my best Biggles-like manner, I turned to a nervous-looking black lady and said: 'It's all right, he's gone now'. She replied: 'Actually, it wasn't me that he was after. It was this lady.'

This other black lady turned to me with a great white-toothed grin: 'Oh, you did not have to worry about me, Sir. I was quite capable of looking after myself.' There was no doubt that this was true. She could certainly have demolished my man very effectively. In my prime, when I boxed for my school, I could have not gone three rounds against her – indeed, I never would have had to do so, because I boxed at either mosquito-weight or paper-weight, and she was definitely in the heavy-weight class.

So, I trudged home, swathes of my coat flapping in the icy wind, shedding from time to time bits of its curious Chinese stuffing. When I informed my family of this episode, my wife felt I had struck a blow against racialism, my fifteen-year-old son thought it was the funniest story he had heard for a long time, and my ten-year-old daughter assured me that God would be very pleased with me.

MAX BYGRAVES

I wanna tell you a sick joke
There is no socialized medicine in the United States, a common cold treated by the local GP could cost about $200, a broken arm could set you back $1,000 and if you die! It could ruin you!

So before I tell you this story, will you bear in mind that some doctors in the States can tell exactly how long you are going to be ill just by feeling your wallet.

A few years ago I left San Francisco to go to Los Angeles. I rented a car and went on the scenic route along the coast. About ten miles outside L.A. I got a nose bleed; after using a full box of Kleenex tissues it still kept bleeding. I was due to make a television appearance on a chat show that same afternoon, so I began to get a little worried.

As luck would have it, I spied a large red cross above a sign that said HOSPITAL, asking motorists 'not to honk horns'.

I drove up to the front door of what looked like a small cottage hospital.

There was a nun seated at the reception desk, she said 'Hi – I'm Sister Rabinowitz'.

'Sister Rabinowitz? Are you a real nun?'

She smiled, 'I was in the chorus of "Sound of Music" for three years.' She asked me what my name was, I told her, she then wrote it down and said 'Next of kin?'

I said, 'What do you want next of kin for – I'm not going to die.'

She smiled again, 'Nobody said you are going to die – it's about time our luck changed.'

I could see I was getting nowhere with this jester so I said, 'Can I see the doctor?'

'Oh' she cried, 'he wants to see the doctor – we've got a Texan oil millionaire here – Doctor!' She slapped a small brass bell as she said 'Doctor' and a door to her left opened immediately to reveal a replica of Groucho Marx. He was dressed in medic's whites with a stethoscope around his neck; his eyebrows never seemed to descend which gave him a permanently surprised look. 'Have you checked this guy's credentials?' he asked the nun. She assured him I was O.K. He then gave me a new box of tissues and told me to wait in a small waiting-room. Inside the waiting-room was a Coca Cola machine, I fished for a quarter and put it into the machine but nothing happened; no bottle of Coke appeared. As it was the only quarter

I had, I decided to sit there, stemming the flow of blood with tissues and hoping that Groucho would not be too long.

After about ten minutes another medic, in whites but without a stethoscope, walked into the waiting-room. He fiddled with the machine, took out a bunch of keys, emptied all the quarters into his pocket and offered me a bottle of Coke. He noticed my bloodied tissues and said, 'Got a nosebleed?' I said I had. He said, 'I use to get that – my wife stopped it in seconds.'

'How'd she do that?' I asked.

'She puts a bottle of ice-cold Coke on the back of my neck – let me try it.'

He bent my head forward and put the ice-cold bottle on my neck – the bleeding stopped immediately.

'Hey that's wonderful,' I cried joyfully, 'How much do I owe you, Doctor?'

He seemed as happy as I was. 'That's alright,' he said, 'You don't owe me anything – besides I'm not the Doctor, I'm the Coca Cola man and I came to fix the machine.'

I made my exit with some garbled explanation to the nun that I couldn't wait any longer, and drove on to L.A.

The moral of this story is, if you are in America and ever get a nose bleed – don't go to a doctor – find the Coca Cola man.

JOHN GIELGUD

King George V, surprised to find himself on one of his morning walks accompanied by a strange detective, enquired brusquely what had become of his usual officer. On being told the regular man was ill, the King enquired what was the matter with him. 'Oh, the universal complaint I understand, Sir,' the new man replied.

On the following morning, Queen Mary was walking in the grounds with her lady-in-waiting, and mentioned she had heard that the King's detective was not well. 'What is the matter with him?' she asked. 'A severe case of haemorrhoids, I believe, Ma'am.'

'Ah,' remarked the Queen briskly, 'how unfortunate. But why did the King tell me it was the clap?'

GEOFFREY BOYCOTT

As a professional cricketer, to be forced to sit and watch your own team score a rare victory over Australia with your arm in a sling is not a subject for hilarity. When the team that England had been trying to vanquish for twelve years was finally beaten, all I could think of was – I wish I'd been out there. The year was 1971: the place Sydney: the prize the Ashes.

Prior to 1971 England had only twice been victorious: in 1933 with Douglas Jardine as captain; and 1959 when they were led by Len Hutton. We seemed fated never to win again, but in 1971 with Ray Illingworth as our captain our luck appeared to change. It had been an excellent tour for the team and I had been on fine form. In fact, it even looked as if I might beat Wally Hammond's record for the most runs ever scored in an Australian summer. As we approached the last Test Match in the seven-run test series, I needed another eighteen runs to beat the record.

Prior to the Test Match we had to play a one-day match against Western Australia – the Australian Gillette Cup champions – and the conditions were far from ideal. Because of torrential rain, the ground had been covered with tarpaulin and when the pitch was eventually uncovered it was very

green, grassy and had sweated a lot. With the third ball of the innings Graham McKenzie 'dug one in' and it reared up at me. I raised my arms to protect my face and the ball hit me on the left forearm. A crack resounded across the field ('We could even hear it in the dressing room' the lads claimed later). In a lot of pain I was promptly whisked off to hospital where an X-ray confirmed my arm was broken.

A few days later I was back at the ground for the final Test Match, although this time confined to a spectator's seat where I could sit with my arm in a sling watching while my own team battled on to pluck the Ashes from the Australians. As the moment of victory approached, my feelings of personal disappointment at not being able to play an active role in the match gave way to a tremendous sense of excitement: I relished the triumph as much as any other member of the team.

Looking back on the experience and recalling the time it took for my arm to heal (I was unable to play for three and a half months), and the exercises and therapy I had to undergo, I can only say how much I sympathize with those whose injuries are permanent. I was lucky my injury, though badly timed, was at least temporary, and since that accident I have enjoyed two more tours of Australia. I now appreciate fully how determined and admirable are those people who have suffered permanent injury and yet still manage to find humour in their disablement.

LEN MURRAY

The world keeps rolling along

So this, I thought, is the end of the world for me – and for the world. My first reaction to a minor heart attack in June 1976 was to feel sorry for myself. In fact, it was one of the best things that could have happened to me.

I had been up to the neck, sometimes higher, in discussions with the Government and unions, engaged in a seemingly endless round of meetings, often stretching into the night, all over the country (I was in Scarborough when I had the attack). I was indeed suffering from the whole syndrome so beloved by 'busy' people.

It took a heart attack to make me realize that what was wrong was my belief, or rather my illusion, that if I stopped running the world would stop revolving on its axis. In fact, the world did not stop while I was in bed – it just went on without me to push it round. Best of all, they held a Special Trades Union Congress without my being there, and overwhelmingly approved an agreement we had reached with the Government. That was most salutary. Even better was the advice I received from a friend. 'Stop and smell the flowers sometimes' he wrote.

So since then I have tried strolling in Epping Forest before breakfast, looking at the beeches – reminding myself that they will be there long after I have gone – watching the grass grow. Busy? Yes, but not making a fetish or a virtue of it, remembering, even at the most difficult times, that so many people are so much worse off than I am, grateful for a timely lesson about arrogance and

humility.

> 'Ye fearful saints, fresh courage take,
> The clouds ye so much dread
> Are big with mercy, and will break
> In blessings on your head.'

CLIFF RICHARD

Despite strange and unfounded rumours that I face my public with a facelift and a colostomy bag, thankfully my only recurring health hazard is a dodgy disc – spinal not vinyl!

Several times over the past ten years or so, the so-called Peter Pan of Pop has sung away in front of concert audiences and TV cameras, conscious that one false move could well leave him looking more like a crippled geriatric. There was one whole BBC TV series I had to endure with the support of a high stool and a very un-hip corset. Maybe it was all that knee-shaking in the days of 'Move It', when a couple of vertebrae did just that. Certainly, according to X-rays, there is a tiny segment of the spine that isn't quite the shape it should be, and that presents a permanent potential hazard.

Nowadays, however, I am ultra-sensitive to any early warning signals and, at the first twinge, I abandon my comfortable bed and take to the bedroom carpet, with the aid of half a dozen blankets. Usually three or four nights of relatively minor discomfort do the trick and whatever was on its way out thinks better of it. I've only experienced that totally crippled state a couple of

times – once while I was soaking up the sun in Madeira, and the other during a Land-Rover safari in Southern Sudan. The latter, I hasten to add, is not recommended!

Relatively speaking, I am well aware that I have

escaped lightly so far but, even so, I reckon I know enough about suspect backs to identify enthusiastically with this little book, hoping that any proceeds will push forward the efforts of the International Spinal Research Trust.

WILLIAM RODGERS

Despite an early addiction to the silent movies – Mack Sennett, the Keystone Cops, Buster Keaton – I have never been an enthusiast for the banana skin. Cracked heads and broken limbs don't bring amusement but a shiver. The limp and the shuffle are disabling even to those who are temporarily afflicted. They become less than themselves, not taken quite so seriously in an impatient world.

So, to me the 'bad luck' was not to be a joke but an embarrassment, reducing the sufferer's effectiveness in a non-specific way without justifying their absence of excusing their behaviour. Like a toothache, or hayfever when the pollen count is high, it was part of the human condition. We had to learn to live with it.

For this reason, my own experience was devastating. There was no dramatic moment, no heroic act for which I paid the penalty. I had neither tried to run a marathon nor climb a mountain. It was the day after Christmas, a leisurely time of rest and slow reflection. But it happened – the sharp stab in the lower back, the inability to move except in agony. I assumed it would pass, like the tingle from a bruised funny-bone or the gasp provoked by the crick-in-the-neck. There was no such luck.

The hurt did not ease: it worsened. The paralysis caused by pain seemed complete.

By the standards of many people, my misfortune was short-lived. I lay on my back on my bed and my doctor said I should stay there. I could sleep and think and read, but even writing was a hardship. It was a period to sort out the confusions of the mind, take stock, make decisions and chart a new course. Whatever the physiological explanations, my 'bad back' was a symptom, enforcing a breathing space that might lead to its cure.

After a few days, I could roll out of bed and in a fortnight I could walk. In a month I could move relatively easily, although still inclined to be tired. I had worked out my future and resolved the worst of my conflicts. I had made my choice and was ready to implement it.

For over thirty years I have lived and worked in one political party, making many friendships and sharing much excitement. To leave it was deeply traumatic. But I had crossed over and the pain of leaving was behind me.

GODFREY SMITH

The first problem was to decide which affliction to write about. Apart from a nose dented honourably on the rugby field long ago, and a finger joint dislocated in the boxing ring, any physical misfortunes seemed mainly confined to a general collapse of the abdominal wall and the usual dandruff. I was mulling over the problem as I set out to the hop in our village hall – and in no time at all was sitting in the casualty ward of the local hospital having my leg swathed in a thirty-foot long surgical bandage.

It was an honourable wound. I had been quietly supping my beer and watching the dancing when they struck up the Can-Can, and I was yanked on to the floor to join in. Nimbly throwing my legs in the air with the best of them, I was suddenly doubled over as a hideous twang ran through me from ankle to knee and the tendon packed in. I knew exactly how sprinters feel who are well on the way to shattering the world record for the two hundred metres when that elastic band in the legs suddenly gives way and they go down like a nine-pin.

For me it was not only character-forming to be hobbling around on a crutch all that week with my gammy leg. It was also a sorely needed alibi. For I have been known to hobble much of late, and I can't truthfully put it down to that piece of shrapnel I bought at the Anzio beach-head. No, my trouble is an ancient one. It was known to the Greeks and the Romans. It afflicts men rather than women, and usually strikes them in middle age. It arrives mysteriously and without warning; it goes in the same way. It manifests itself in an exquisitely tender big toe which cannot in any circumstances be bent. Steps must be taken stiff-legged, one at a time. Progress is slow. The slightest bang is the purest agony. It is the traditional trouble of brick-faced colonels and country squires. It can be hereditary or it can be brought on, or so they say, by looking on the wine when it is red. Imagine how glad I was, then, to have a genuine reason for hobbling on one leg. No longer could they gossip, as I shuffled by in the *bodegas* of

Fleet Street, Godders is gouty again. I had fallen in a genuine battle.

NIGEL HAVERS

Every young actor in London had heard about David Puttnam's proposed film, *Chariots of Fire*. It was a rare chance to be involved in an all-British film about loyalty and gamesmanship, set in the roaring twenties. There were endless auditions and screen tests, usually with your best mates wondering whether you were all up for the same role. Oh, what a nightmare! And they said that films were fun!

By sheer good fortune I was called by Hugh Hudson, the director, to the Chiswick Sports Centre to demonstrate my running ability. It was a cold miserable February afternoon. I'd even bought myself a very expensive pair of running shoes with spikes, just in case. . . . In for a penny in for a pound, I thought. We were greeted by an International Olympic coach, Tom McNab, who told us quite sternly to run round the training area FOUR times, just to warm up. Those of us who weren't sick survived the next round, and with an empty stomach on my side I survived, to be cast as Lord Andrew Lindsay.

To celebrate my extraordinary luck, my agent took my wife and me out to dinner – it turned out to be the last time I touched a cigarette or a drink for far too long! The very next day I was under contract, and that meant being a 'good boy', no smokes, no booze and in bed by ten o'clock.

Tom McNab reappeared on the scene and, oh boy, what a taskmaster he turned out to be. Of course, it had to be Havers who had the job of becoming an Olympic hurdler. Why me? The first week I had to be lifted out of bed in the morning and at costume-fitting I could hardly try on a pair of trousers without screams of agony. I pounded the streets for miles every evening and spent hours of the day trying to tackle those damned hurdles, believing that I was the next Alan Pascoe. It was rather like learning to drive – thinking you'll never do it. But suddenly one afternoon in some strange training centre in East London it all started to fall into place. God had smiled and those hurdles were fun to 'snap' over as Tom McNab said they would be. It was late in the afternoon and Tom had said for once that I hadn't been as spastic as usual, in fact I was beginning to look quite alright. For the first time I felt confident.

'I want to do it one more time' I said, and off I went. I hit the first hurdle at about ninety miles an hour and did a spin that Robin Cousins would have been proud of. In an attempt to keep upright, my left arm touched the ground with such force that my shoulder blade ended up in the middle of my back and my left wrist cracked like a rifle shot. Was this the end I thought? Was I a broken man? Having come so far, for it to end like this was absurd. Trainers, coaches, athletes all came from nowhere and none of them could tell me whether I had broken anything. Even if I had, no one was going to know. I wasn't going to let a chance like this disappear for a broken bone!

Tom McNab bundled a white shaking torso into his car, told me to eat a Mars Bar – 'it's good for the adrenalin' – and off we set in search for the nearest hospital. Three hours later we found one, whereupon I was X-rayed and informed that my shoulder was only dislocated (I covered up my wrist). The doctors asked me if I had eaten anything recently.

'Well, just a Mars Bar'.

'Oh no, that means you'll have to wait at least an hour'.

Eventually the general anaesthetic allowed the doctor to re-position my shoulder. As soon as I woke up, I checked my mobility . . . bingo . . . out it went again. Oh God, the same thing all over again. This time I woke up to find myself strapped to the bed. I got home at midnight, but I was still Lord Andrew Lindsay.

The phone rang at nine o'clock the next morning.

'You're alright I trust,' said Tom McNab.

'Of course,' I squeaked.

'Good, now, I'll see you at ten o'clock, we've got to tackle six hurdles today.'

No wonder somebody said . . . never put your daughter on the stage Mrs Worthington!